21 Days

Stephanie Medina Torres

BookLeaf Publishing

India | USA | UK

Presentation by *BookLeaf Publishing*

Web: www.bookleafpub.com

E-mail: info@bookleafpub.com

ISBN: 978-93-5761-210-4

First edition 2022

DEDICATION

I dedicate this to my husband, my children and
to memory of my father.

Jumping Jacks

As the warm summer sun, shone down on your face,
you picked up the Jacks with such subtle grace.

First one jack then two, three and then four,
You swept them all up, till there were no more.

"Sit Indian style" you told me, "I'll teach you how,
bounce your red ball and scoop them up now!"

You twirled and you danced them across on the floor,
Ballerinas you called them and twirled some more.

Have you Ever

Have you ever sat in darkness and let yourself just cry?
When you think of all the painful things and ask yourself, just why?

Just why was it so easy to hurt me and to go?
And now you are a stranger, that I no longer know.

You picked up and you moved on, without a single trace.
My mother's love, instantly gone, right before my face.

Have you ever sat in loneliness and let yourself just cry?
When you've lost someone, you truly loved and couldn't say goodbye.

Low and Slow

3

The whaling of our sirens, as down the street we
go.
Throwing up our "V" signs, cruising low and
slow.
You hear us before you see us, when we roll up
in a line.
Our bombitas fresh and shined up, looking
pretty fine.
United is what our club is, a family and it shows,
Viejitos Car Club Worldwide, so everybody
knows!

The Gates from Heaven

The gates from Heaven are open, there's a cloud
with an empty space,
awaiting your arrival and the smile on your face.

God has a golden halo and a pair of fluffy wings,
Welcome home to Heaven, is what the Angel
sings.

Living with the angels, is where you now will
be,
being held inside the good Lords arms, for all
eternity.

Without a Sign

Without a sign or warning, God came to take
you home,
with all the gardens of Heaven, ready for you to
roam.
Your time to rest has come now, to go and to be
free,
a new life filled with beauty, is what you soon
will see.
Go and find our loved ones now, and hold your
baby boy,
They've been waiting your arrival with
anticipated joy.
Until the day we meet again, in Heaven up
above,
I know you'll be right next to me, still showing
me your love.

My Forever

The day you came into this world, my forever
changed and the life that I had always known,
has now been rearranged.

Ten tiny little fingers, ten tiny perfect toes, this
love that has filled my being, only a mother
knows!

Your eyes filled with pure innocence as they
peer into my heart, please God protect my
newborn love and never let us part.

Some Sisters

I've always been so jealous when I look around
and see, how close some sisters live their lives
but that's not you and me.

I've always wondered what I did to be pushed so
far away, to come to this point where I look at
you and find no words to say.

I used to want to be like you, my only sister and
my rock, but I've shamed you somewhere
throughout our lives, and now we don't even
talk.

I used to wish I would hear from you, that you'd
call me on the phone, but I've given up after all
these years of being all alone.

I'm happy you found your sisters now, at least
one of us can see, what it feels like to have a
sister, even if it isn't me.

Who's House is this

Whose house is this I'm walking through; I've seen it in my dreams. But today I'm lost and all alone, a nightmare so it seems.

The pictures that are on the wall, of the loved ones in my life. From all the time I spent with my children, to the time I became a wife.

Where have all my kids gone; none of them are here. In my dreams, I don't have to look, for all of them are near.

Oh wait, that's not a dream, they are memories in my heart. The reason that my kids are gone, is because we had to part.

They've moved away to live their lives and there's something they should know, no matter how proud I am of you, my heart misses you so!

God Sent

I cannot call you just a friend, the truth is you're
much more. You're the person that God sent me,
when I felt my heart was tore.

It was torn and bled from a painful past, that I
once had to live, where I was filled with so
much anger, I had no love to give.

You took me from that darkness and showed me
I was loved, stand next to me with
encouragement any time push comes to shove.

You've shown me I could live my life, without
people who cause me pain. You are the calm to
my storm, and you always keep me sane.

Boo

Have you ever had your heart, just up and melt away, when you find a special someone with one special thing to say?

Your breath is taken straight from you, your stomach in a knot, all the troubles you were having, you suddenly have forgot.

A tiny little person, so gentle and so sweet, from the top of her precious head to her dancing little feet.

Boo is what I call her, Grandma she calls me. Oh, I cannot wait to see what she will be!

This Road

To wake up next to you each day, is a blessing in
my life. Almost as much of a blessing, as being
called your wife.

You've held me up through thick and thin,
through good times and through bad. My love,
my life, my happiness, best gift I've ever had.

You save me from the monsters that wander in
my head. Awake a part of my soul, that's often
lost and dead.

You remind of my happiness and the blessings
that we've won. We're going to make it together,
on this road that we are on.

Courage

This never-ending road I'm on, is mine to call
my own, for it was me who stood up and fought
for myself, even if I fought alone.

Someone had to stop him, that someone would
be me. I was going to expose him, for all the
world to see.

I sat up in a court room, having to look out at my
dad, when I spoke about the things he did, it
took everything I had.

I knew I had to stop him though, put this
monster in his place. So, I pulled out all my
courage and I looked him in the face.

A slap on the wrist is what he got, for what he
did to me, but when his time on this earth is
over, God's judgement he will see.

Fire in the Sky

The colors all around me, look like the sky is on fire, as the sun sets deep into the night, the mountains they seem higher.

The red and orange colors, gently kiss the hardened ground, illuminating the beauty in everything around.

Darkness soon will follow, and nighttime will be near, so enjoy the fire in the sky, while its beauty is still here.

Tell Me

Tell me that you love me and tell me that it's
true, that everything you mean to me, I mean
that to you.

Tell me you will never leave, that together we'll
grow old, that our love will make us rich inside,
as if we just struck gold.

Tell me that you trust me and what I'd do for
you, for it's you and I together, the world against
us two.

You are the One

15

All my wishful destinations and things I want to
do, have one thing all in common, that one
thing, it is you.

You never let me stand alone, you are always by
my side, protect me from my madness, reason
my darkness died.

Not every day is perfect and not every day is
fair, but no matter what the next day brings, I
know you will be there.

All of my greatest memories of things that we
have done, have proven what I've always known,
for me you are the one.

I Wish

I wish I could stop loving you, the way you did
with me, I'm tired of being so miserable for all
the world to see.

I want to wake up happy and know I'm not alone
but you up and went away, to live life on your
own.

I gave you all I possibly could, with my
damaged heart, yet still I sit here without you,
for now we live apart.

I wish I could stop wanting you and realize my
own worth, for I am loved, and I am needed and
it's time for my rebirth.

No Return

When you're taken past the point of light, the
point of no return, it's a place you do not want to
be, an escape is what you yearn.

People, you no longer trust, no matter where you
go. For they turned their heads, closed their
eyes, pretended not to know.

They say that it's not happening, turn their backs
and walk away. Because that's what clears their
conscience, to carry on each day.

When you're taken beyond the point of light,
your innocence you lose. Will you be a victim
or a survivor, that's for you to choose!

Angel on My Tree

Christmas soon is coming; I wish that you were
here, but I see the signs you leave me and know
that you are near.

Your picture is lit with gold and wings, the
Angel on our tree. Oh, if you were here with us,
how different this would be.

I miss you so much daddy, things will never be
the same, my heart still feels so broken, even
just to speak your name.

You always were my hero and me, your princess
they would say, so in honor of the life you lived,
I will continue on each day.

Gramita

I shed a tear for you today but not because I'm
sad. I was thinking of the memories of the good
times that we had.

From camping at the river and picking pinons
under the trees, to playing with Raggedy Ann
and cleaning my scraped knees.

Christmas Eve and Thanksgiving will never be
the same, but we'll carry on your traditions and
often speak your name.

Your acceptance was never ending; your heart
knew nothing but love. Our very own special
Angel, sent from up above.

I'm happy you're at peace now, all your pains
and fears are gone. You're dancing up in
Heaven; Eternal life is what you've won.

I have faith that we will meet again, and that day
will be so great, for the day that God will call
me home; you will be with him at that gate.

Now spread your wings and fly away, your soul
has been set free and when I see a butterfly, I
will know you are here with me.

My Hero

21

To say you were my hero, falls short of how I feel, but I cannot find the words to say, for this all seems so unreal.

How is it that my daddy's gone, there's no way this could be, please tell me this is all a dream and you're still here with me.

I need more time to tell you how sorry that I am, to kiss you and to hug you, to have hold my hand.

God's whispering in my ear now, this is not a dream, and this is true, but he says its warm in Heaven and he's getting ready to go fishing with you.

He says Chris is packed and ready, to the lake that you will go, you're at peace now, no more pain inside, in my heart daddy this i know.

God's Gentle Grace

22

As the lights from your room, shone down on
your face, you took your last breath, with God's
gentle grace.

First one week, then two, three and then four,
you fought it your hardest till there was no more.

I'll always be left with the question of how,
instead of being with here with me, you're my
angel now.